What If ?

BE WELL PRESS

Encouraging others...one page at a time

ISBN 979-8-9889161-0-9

Dear Readers,

I am excited to share with you my book, "What If?" In this story children and adolescents will learn useful techniques for managing anxious thoughts. Negative thoughts that focus on the future can create worry, frustration and other big feelings. Challenging our thoughts with questions such as: What is the worst-case scenario in this situation, what is the best-case outcome and the most likely thing to happen; these questions can help us stay rooted in the present moment.

Many of the concepts described in this story are based on a well-known approach to psychotherapy, Cognitive Behavioral Therapy (CBT). Originally developed by psychiatrist Dr. Aaron Beck, CBT focuses on noticing negative thoughts and understanding their connection to feelings and behaviors. This helps us become aware of our negative thinking patterns and teaches us to reframe our thoughts, which helps us experience more peaceful moments.

I hope this fun story helps the children in your life. I would love for this story to make them smile while learning skills that could ease their anxiety and help in moments of big feelings. Be Well!

Peace, Laura Hernandez

Laura Hernandez, Ph.D.,LPC-S
Licensed Professional Counselor- Supervisor

Ages 6 and up

Sometimes my brain asks a question,
about the tomorrows that lie ahead.
It makes it difficult to concentrate,
because the answers I often dread.

The question brings me to the future,
a place I cannot control.
It comes up with the worst possible conclusion,
to a story that hasn't been told.

It makes my brain feel anxious, worried, and afraid.
All because I'm fretting about a future yet to be made.

The question I am referring to, we all know it well.
"What if ?" applies to every situation,
the worst scenario it will often tell.

What if ?

What if...
The other kids won't play with me,
and my post doesn't get any likes.
I don't get invited to the party and I tumble off my bike!

What if...

I jumped on my trampoline, so high, to the moon I flew.
You see it's often thinking of things that aren't even true!

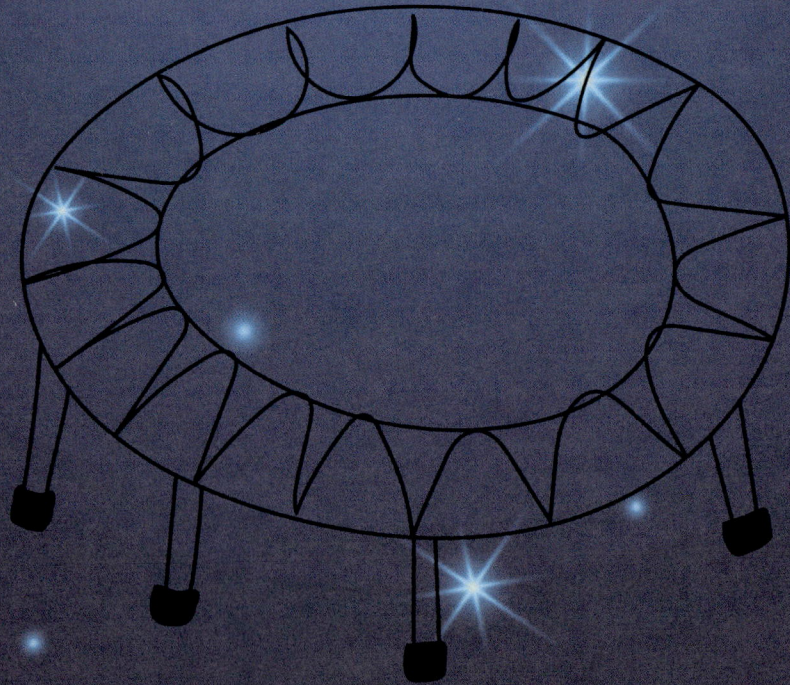

What if....

I get a bad grade because I forget all the
teacher has taught.

My brain is just so tired!

All these thoughts...I'm so distraught!

Sometimes our brain gets carried away
with thoughts not true or real.
We get caught up in the worst case scenario,
thinking, "Hey brain, what's the deal?!"

Our brain finds problems to keep us safe.
It prepares us for what's up ahead.
From "Will I oversleep and miss my ride to school?"
To "Watch out! There's a lion that hasn't been fed!"

It's really quite ridiculous, if you take a minute and think.
Could all these worst scenarios happen?
That would really stink!

But if we take a moment, to breathe and reason through,
another thing may happen, something different may come true.

Our biggest fear is the focus
but other choices can be.
Challenge your thoughts, look at the big picture
and there may be more to see.

We may see other options,
the "What if?" question in another light.
Something quite spectacular,
let's think with all our might!

What if ?

What if....
I am successful and my friends are kind!
I stay healthy and when testing,
all I studied comes to mind.

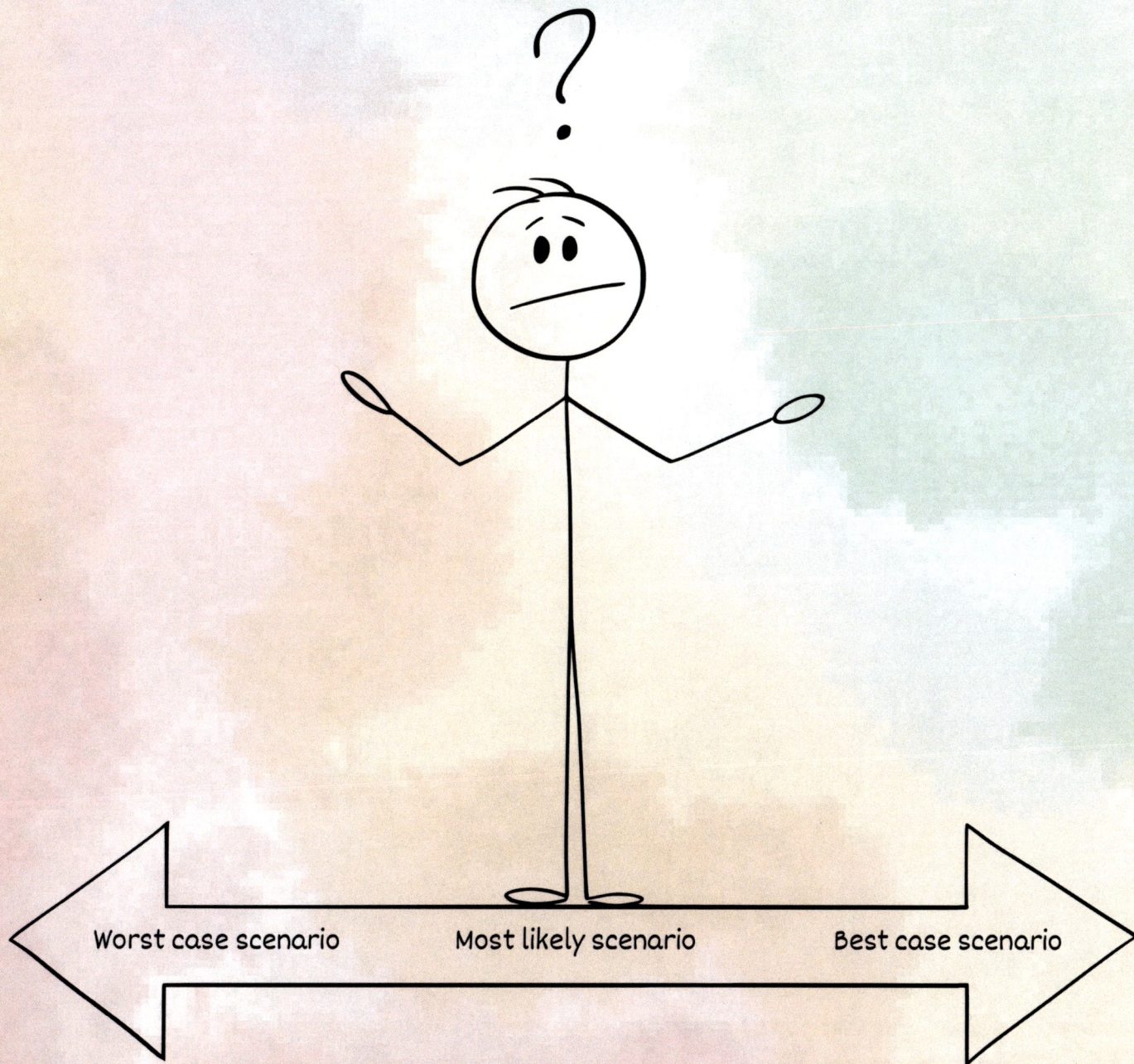

Worst case scenario   Most likely scenario   Best case scenario

See it really is quite simple. Just train your brain to see, that each time you think the worst, another side may be.

There's a different way to think of things.
Challenge your thoughts instead.
Is this the only thing that can happen- the very thing we dread?

To see and explore the bright side, ask "What if ?" again,
but this time look a little closer.
You may even help a friend!

Looking for the good things, even when they're hard to find,
answering the "What if ?" question- really exploring your mind.

This is the key to a peaceful mind
because the future we can't control,
but the present moment that we live in,
is the one that we can mold.

If we live in the future,
we can feel nervous and worry,
but returning to the present
is where we write our story.

THE END

About the Author

Dr. Laura Hernandez lives in New Orleans, Louisiana with her husband, son, two daughters and their pup, Arby. She worked in a school setting for 19 years as a teacher, administrator and counselor. Throughout that time, she loved helping children and adolescents in many stages of development including early childhood, elementary, middle school and high school. During the COVID shutdown Dr. Hernandez experienced the increase in anxiety with her children and noticed that many families had similar struggles. She decided to open her private practice, Be Well NOLA Counseling, where she counsels children, teens and adults.

She loves writing stories that bring children joy and supporting their mental health needs.

www.bewellnola.com   Instagram: @nolabewell

Check out another great book by
Dr. Laura Hernandez:
"The Tootin' Golden" a story about
friendship and calming anxious thoughts.
Available at bewellpress.com

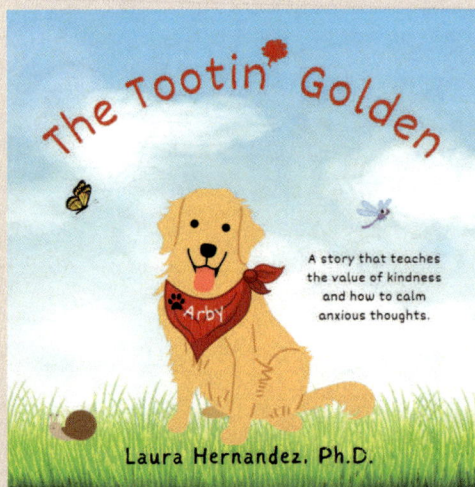

Made in the USA
Middletown, DE
21 August 2023